MACMILLAN READE[illegible]

PRE-INTERMEDIATE LEVEL

RACHEL BLADON

The Story of the Olympics: An Unofficial History

MACMILLAN

MACMILLAN READERS

PRE-INTERMEDIATE LEVEL

Founding Editor: John Milne

The Macmillan Readers provide a choice of enjoyable reading materials for learners of English. The series is published at six levels – Starter, Beginner, Elementary, Pre-intermediate, Intermediate and Upper.

Level Control

Information, structure and vocabulary are controlled to suit the students' ability at each level.

The number of words at each level:

Starter	about 300 basic words
Beginner	about 600 basic words
Elementary	about 1100 basic words
Pre-intermediate	about 1400 basic words
Intermediate	about 1600 basic words
Upper	about 2200 basic words

Vocabulary

Some difficult words and phrases in this book are important for understanding the story. Some of these words are explained in the story, some are shown in the pictures and others are marked with a number like this: …[3]. Words with a number are explained in the *Glossary* at the end of the book.

Answer Keys

Answer Keys for the *Points for Understanding* and *Exercises* sections can be found at www.macmillanenglish.com/readers.

Audio Download

There is an audio download available to buy for this title. Visit www.macmillanenglish.com/readers for more information.

Contents

A Glossary of Sports

archery the sport of shooting *arrows* – thin straight sticks with a sharp point at one end and feathers at the other – from a *bow* – a weapon made from a curved piece of wood or metal

athletics sports such as running or jumping

baseball a game played by two teams of nine players who score points by hitting a ball with a bat and then running around four bases

basketball a game played by two teams of five players who score points by throwing a ball through a net

BMX cycling a sport in which eight people ride special bicycles with small wheels around a track that has bends and small hills. The fastest person is the winner.

bobsledding the sport of racing down a track over snow and ice in a small vehicle for two or more people

boxing a sport in which two people fight each other wearing large leather gloves on their hands

canoeing a sport in which you travel over water in a light narrow boat which you push through the water using a short pole with two flat ends

croquet a sport in which players hit balls through curved pieces of metal using wooden hammers with long handles

fencing the sport of fighting with a weapon with a short handle and a long sharp blade

football a game in which two teams of eleven players kick a ball and try to score goals

gymnastics a sport in which athletes perform physical exercises that involve bending and balancing

handball a sport in which two teams of players use their hands to pass a ball and try to score goals

hockey a sport that is played on grass by two teams of eleven players. They try to score goals by hitting a ball with a stick that has a curved end.

ice hockey a sport that is played on ice by two teams of six players. The players use long sticks to try to hit a small round flat object into the other team's goal.

ice-skating the sport of moving on ice wearing special shoes with a thin metal blade on the bottom. In *figure-skating*, you have to jump, spin and move round the ice in a particular way.

judo a sport in which you fight using balance and the weight of your body to throw your opponent to the ground

luge the sport of racing down a track over ice in a small vehicle for one or two people in which you lie down and control the vehicle with your feet and arms

rowing a sport in which you move a boat through water using poles with flat ends called *oars*

sailing the sport or activity of travelling across water in a small boat that uses a sail or sails to move along

shooting a sport in which competitors fire guns to hit targets

softball a sport similar to baseball but played on a smaller field and with a larger, softer ball

taekwondo a sport in which two people try to hit each other with their hands and feet

track sports such as running and jumping

triple jump a sport in which you first jump forwards on one leg, jump again on the other leg, and jump a third time using both legs

volleyball a sport in which two teams use their hands and arms to hit a ball to each other over a high net

weightlifting the sport of lifting heavy weights

wrestling a sport in which two people fight by holding each other with their arms and trying to push or throw each other to the ground. In *freestyle wrestling*, fighters can use their arms and their legs.

Summer Olympic Games, 1896 to Today

		Number of competitors	Number of countries	Number of events
1896	Athens, Greece	241	14	43
1900	Paris, France	997	26	95
1904	St Louis, USA	651	13	91
1908	London, Great Britain	2,008	22	110
1912	Stockholm, Sweden	2,407	28	102
1916	The Games were cancelled			
1920	Antwerp, Belgium	2,626	29	154
1924	Paris, France	3,089	44	126
1928	Amsterdam, Holland	2,883	46	109
1932	Los Angeles, USA	1,332	37	117
1936	Berlin, Germany	3,963	49	129
1940	The Games were cancelled.			
1944	The Games were cancelled.			
1948	London, Great Britain	4,104	59	136
1952	Helsinki, Finland	4,955	69	149
1956	Melbourne, Australia	3,314	72	145
1960	Rome, Italy	5,338	83	150
1964	Tokyo, Japan	5,151	93	163
1968	Mexico City, Mexico	5,516	112	172
1972	Munich, Germany	7,134	121	195

1976	Montreal, Canada	6,084	92	198
1980	Moscow, Soviet Union	5,179	80	203
1984	Los Angeles, USA	6,829	140	221
1988	Seoul, South Korea	8,391	159	237
1992	Barcelona, Spain	9,356	169	257
1996	Atlanta, USA	10,318	197	271
2000	Sydney, Australia	10,651	199	300
2004	Athens, Greece	10,625	201	301
2008	Beijing, China	10,942	204	302
2012	London, Great Britain			
2016	Rio de Janeiro, Brazil			

1

The Olympics Today

Thousands of athletes[1] and spectators[2] are waiting, excited. They are in a new stadium[3] in one of the most important cities in the world. Then an athlete stands up. He promises that the thousands of athletes in the stadium will play their sport fairly[4]. He promises that they will try their hardest for their sport and for their country. There is music, singing, dancing and fireworks[5]. The Olympic Games have begun!

The Summer Olympics are one of the biggest sports events[6] in the world and they are held only once every four years. More than ten thousand athletes from around the world come to the Summer Olympic Games and compete[7] in more than three hundred events, in twenty-six different sports. There are running and swimming races[8], athletics and gymnastics events, and many other games are played, including basketball and football. In every event, the winners are given medals[9]: gold for first place, silver for second and bronze for third. Many of the athletes who compete become famous in their own country and around the world.

This book is mainly about the Summer Olympic Games. The Summer Olympics are held in a specially chosen international city. The Winter Olympic Games are smaller. They are held in a different place, two years after the Summer Olympics. The most important Winter events are in sports like skiing, ice-skating and bobsledding. In the same places and in the same years, there are also Summer and Winter Paralympics – Olympic Games for people with a disability[10]. In 2010 the first ever Youth Olympics were also held.

A team[11] of athletes from nearly every country in the world comes to the Olympics. Millions of people watch the Games on television. Because the Games are so big and so important, many countries want to host them – to hold them in their country.

The Olympic Games are organized[12] by the International Olympic Committee[13], or IOC. The IOC chooses the best place for the Summer and Winter Olympics every four years. Committees for the different sports and for the host country help to organize the Games. There is a lot of work to do when a country hosts the Olympics. Often new stadiums and swimming pools are needed and the host country also has to build an Olympic village where the athletes sleep, eat and relax during the Games. The host country often has to improve roads and public transport – that means more buses and trains. It is important that athletes and spectators can travel easily to and from the Games. Hosting the Olympics is very expensive, but the Games can bring a lot of money to the host country. When a country hosts the Olympics, many tourists travel there. People all around the world see and learn about the country.

The very first Olympic Games were held in Greece nearly three thousand years ago. The Olympics have grown and changed a lot since then. Because they are so old and so big, there are many Olympic traditions. The Olympics have their own anthem, or song, and their own special flag. The flag has five coloured rings. Every Olympic Games also has its own mascot – an animal or object that is specially chosen for that year's Games. The mascot is chosen by the host country and is seen in every piece of information about the Olympics that year. Often the mascot is something that makes people think of the host country. For the 2000 Summer Olympics in Sydney, the mascots were three Australian animals. The mascot for the 1980 Olympics in Moscow, Russia, was a bear called Misha.

The first important event of the Olympic Games is when the Olympic torch[14] is lit. The torch is lit in Olympia, the place in

The Olympic flag being carried into the stadium at the 1988 Seoul Games

Greece where the Olympics first began. It is lit several months before the Games start and is then carried by athletes, handed from one to another, across the world. In the months before the 2008 Olympics, the torch travelled 137,000 kilometres! It arrives at the Games during the opening ceremony[15].

The opening ceremony is an important part of the Summer Olympic Games. First there is a parade[16] of all the athletes who are competing in the Games. As the Olympic Games started in Greece, the Greek team is always at the front of the parade. The host team is always at the back. Next there are speeches[17], made by the president of the IOC and the organizer of the games, and then the Olympic anthem is played. After that the Olympic flag is carried into the stadium and put up so everyone can see it. After the flag, the Olympic torch is brought into the stadium. A famous athlete then uses the torch to light the Olympic cauldron[18], which burns until the end of the Games. Some white pigeons[19] are then set free and they fly out of the stadium. This is to show that the Olympic Games are always held in peace[20]. Then, after an athlete and a judge[21] have promised to compete and judge fairly, the host country's national anthem is played. At the end of the opening ceremony there is a wonderful show with music and dancing.

For the next sixteen days, the best sportspeople in the world compete with each other in many different events. Often the weather is much hotter, colder, drier or wetter than in the athletes' own countries. Many of them are thousands of kilometres away from their families and friends. There are always surprises, disappointments[22] and great moments. New records are set when people run or swim faster than ever before, or jump or throw higher or further. Hundreds of medals are awarded and many people become famous for the first time.

At the closing ceremony, the athletes enter the stadium once more, this time not in their national teams but all together. National anthems are played and the host country returns the Olympic flag to the IOC. The flag is then given to the country that will host the next Olympics. The fire in the cauldron is put out and the Games have finished. People must wait another four years for the next Summer Olympic Games.

Lighting the Olympic cauldron at the opening ceremony at the 1988 Seoul Games

2

The First Games

The first Olympic Games were held in Olympia, in Greece, in or around the year 800 BC[23]. At this time, Greece was very important in the world. The Greek world was growing because many Greeks were moving to live in different places around the Mediterranean[24]. Other Greeks travelled to these places to buy and sell things. Greek people also produced beautiful art and wrote many poems and stories.

Greece was made up of different 'city states'. Each city state – a city and the countryside around it – was ruled[25] by a group of rich men. The city states were quite small, but there was often fighting between them.

Greek people loved athletics and the rulers of the city states wanted their men to do as much sport as possible. They knew that men who were athletic could fight better in wars. The Greeks also believed in many different gods[26] and goddesses and had lots of religious[27] ceremonies. Because the Greeks liked sport so much, there were athletics competitions at all the big religious ceremonies. There were even athletics competitions at important funerals[28].

The Greeks told many stories – called myths – about the world around them and the gods they believed in. There are many different myths about how the Olympic Games first began. One myth tells the story that Pelops, the king of Olympia, competed in a chariot[29] race with another king, Oinomaos, because Pelops wanted to marry Oinomaos's daughter. Oinomaos's chariot was broken, so Pelops won the race. Another myth is that the first Olympic Games were funeral games held for Pelops after he died.

When the Olympic Games began, Olympia was in the city

state of Elis in the south-west of Greece, with olive[30] trees and small hills all around. The Olympic Games were held during a religious ceremony for Zeus, the king of the gods, and for Hera, his queen. The first Games that were written about were in 776 BC, but there had probably been Olympic Games long before that year. In 776 BC, the Olympic Games took place on just one day. The only event was a race from one end of the stadium in Olympia to the other, and the runners wore shorts but no shoes. By 724 BC, fifty years later, there were two longer races.

Olympia today

For most athletics competitions, people only came from the city state where they were held. For the first Olympics, the only competitors were men from Elis or city states near Elis. But it did not take long for the Games to become extremely popular all over Greece. About 2,500 years ago, there were four big sports competitions in Greece, including the Olympic Games. Together these four were called the *Panhellenic* Games. People came to compete in them from other parts of Greece. The Olympic Games quickly became the most important of these events and the most popular sports event in the country. Thousands of spectators came from as far away as Spain and Egypt.

Like the modern[31] Olympic Games, the first Olympics were held every four years. The Greeks called this four-year gap between the Games an *Olympiad.* Later, they used the word Olympiad to talk about dates. Someone might say, for example, that they were born in the first year of the third Olympiad.

Before each Olympic Games, men travelled around all the lands belonging to Greece. They told people the dates of the next Games and invited them to come. They also told them that there was now a sacred truce. This meant that it was a time of peace and there could be no wars or fighting until the end of the Olympics. Before and after every Olympic Games, all wars had to stop so that people could travel safely to and from the Games.

There were two kinds of people in Ancient[32] Greece: free men and slaves[33]. Slaves could not do what they wanted. They were owned by the free men and had to work for them. Only free men could compete in the Olympics. Slaves were not allowed[34] to take part[35].

In the early Olympics, only Greek men could compete. Men who wanted to compete had to train[36] for ten months before they could take part. There was a different competition for women, called the *Heraia.* This had three running events for women and girls of different ages. The women and girls wore special short dresses for running.

After the first fifty years of the Olympics, men began to compete naked[37]. The Greeks believed that this made them faster. They also wanted everyone to see the athletes' strong bodies. Only men and unmarried women were allowed to watch the Games. Married women were not allowed to watch. Married women spectators were thrown off the top of Mount Typaeon, a high mountain not far from Olympia.

3

The Ancient Olympics

In 456 BC a new Temple[38] of Zeus was built at Olympia. After this wonderful temple was built, even more people came to the Olympic Games. There was a famous statue[39] of Zeus inside the temple which was 13 metres high, and at every Olympics thousands of people came to see it. Many other buildings were also put up for the Games. Next to the stadium where the running races were held, there was a *hippodrome* for chariot and horse races. There was also a big *palaestra*, or training ground, where athletes could practise and get ready for their events. A hotel was built for the judges and there was also a building for the Olympic Council, which organized the Games. The *prytaneion* was a place where important people and the winning athletes had special dinners. There was a fire there that never went out. The fire was holy – people who believed in God thought it was special and important.

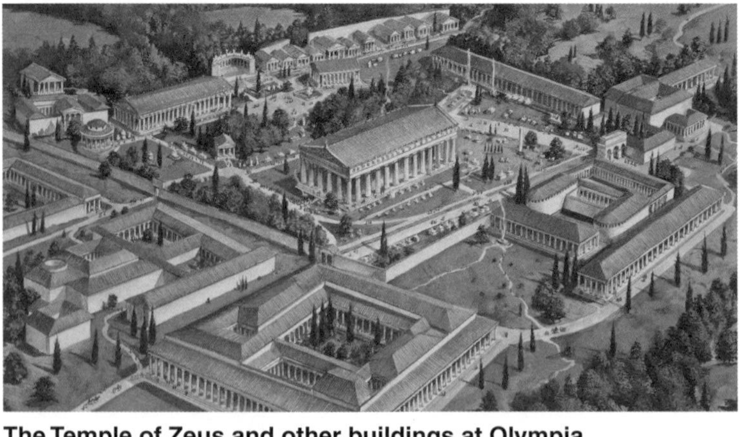

The Temple of Zeus and other buildings at Olympia

Religion was a very important part of the Games and there were lots of ceremonies. Many people thought that the god Zeus himself decided who won each event. There was an oracle at Olympia – people believed that the oracle could tell them the words of the gods. Many athletes went to see the oracle before the Games. They believed the oracle already knew the winners of every event.

By 400 BC the Games lasted for five days. The competitors had to train for many months before they went to the Games. When they arrived in Olympia, they spent another month training together in the *palaestra*. There were a lot of rules for the athletes and they were given only cheese and water at meals. The judges watched the athletes train and then chose the best ones. Only these men could compete in the Games.

On the first day of the Olympics, the athletes registered to show that they were going to compete. They had to promise to follow the rules of the Games.

On the second day, there were chariot races, horse races and the pentathlon. The *tethrippon* – the chariot race – was one of the most popular events. The chariots were pulled by two or four horses and had to go around the hippodrome twelve times. Forty chariots could race at the same time, so chariots often hit each other. The horse races could be dangerous, too. In one of the horse races, the riders had to get off and run behind their horse. Not surprisingly, there were many accidents.

The pentathlon was made up of five different sports. It was one of the hardest events. Athletes had to run, jump and wrestle, and they had to throw a discus (a round stone or piece of metal) and a javelin (a long, thin piece of wood). Only athletes who were very strong did well in the pentathlon.

On the third day of the Olympics, there were track races. The oldest Olympic sport was running and there were now three main races. For the *stade*, athletes had to run on a track from one end of the stadium to the other – a distance of about

Chariot racing

192 metres. For the *diaulos*, they had to run back again as well. For the *dolichos*, they had to run up and down the track between eighteen and twenty-four times. This was a distance of nearly five kilometres. The athletes still did not wear shoes and the track was covered in sand[40]. About forty thousand spectators watched these races from hills around the stadium. The athletes were still naked during the Olympics, but the runners put olive oil on their bodies before a race. This kept their skin clean and made them look strong and healthy.

The fourth day of the Games was for boxing and there were also three wrestling events. In the wrestling, men had to pull their competitor to the ground. They put oil and then sand on their bodies. They could hold their competitors more easily when their bodies were covered in sand. One of the wrestling events was called the *pankration*. In this event, men could not bite[41] or poke out[42] each other's eyes, but they could fight in any other way. Men hit, kicked and broke parts of each other's body. This event often went on for several hours and some competitors died. The fight only ended when one of the competitors said he wanted to stop. Then the other man became the winner.

On the fifth day, prizes were given to the winning competitors. Until the sixth century[43] AD, the only prizes for the winners were crowns[44] made from the branches[45] of a holy olive tree. The Greeks believed that the real prize was trying your hardest and winning at these important Games. In the winner's home city, there were big celebrations[46] and the athlete became a very important person. Often the people of the city gave him free meals for the rest of his life. In some places people pulled down the high walls around their city when one of their men became an Olympic winner. They believed they were safe from attack because such a strong man lived there too.

Because there was no fighting during the Games, Olympia became a very important meeting place for Greek leaders. When there were no wars, it was easier for them to talk together about politics and trade. The Olympic Games also gave the Greeks a strong feeling of unity – of living and working together with each other as one big group.

Many famous people, including Plato and Aristotle, came to watch the Olympic Games. Many athletes also became famous after they became Olympic winners. Milo of Croton, in Italy, and Leonidas of Rhodes were two of the most famous athletes of the ancient Olympics. Milo won the wrestling event six times in the sixth century and Leonidas won all three running events at four different Olympic Games in the second century BC.

In 146 BC, the Romans came to Greece. Under their rule, the Ancient Greek religion became less important in Greece. Other religions were introduced and the strongest of these was Christianity[47]. The Olympic Games went on under Roman rule until 393 AD. In that year, more than a thousand years after the Games first started, the Roman Emperor[48] Theodosius I stopped the Olympics. Theodosius wanted Greece to be a more Christian country and he did not like the religious ceremonies of the Olympics. Thirty years later, the Temple of Zeus was destroyed[49]. Then, because they were not used, the other Olympic buildings slowly fell down and became ruins[50]. Later, during the sixth century, Olympia was hit by two big earthquakes[51]. After this, river floods[52] damaged the ancient buildings and buried[53] them far below the ground.

Fifteen centuries later, in 1875, archeologists[54] began to look for the ruins of Olympia. There, buried under five metres of earth, they found beautiful works of art, statues and the ancient temple of Hera. They even found the ruins of the Olympic stadium.

Today you can still visit the ancient ruins of Olympia. For the 2004 Athens Olympics, the old stadium was rebuilt. Some of the events of the 2004 Games were held there, in the ancient home of the early Olympics.

4

The Start of the Modern Olympics

There were big changes in Greece, and for more than a thousand years there were no Olympic Games. From 1453 the Ottomans, who were powerful people from Turkey, ruled the Greeks. Greece only became independent again in 1829, nearly four hundred years later. At that time, in the 1830s, a few people began to think about the ancient Olympics and they wanted to start the Olympic Games once more.

Panagiotis Soutsos

The first person who talked about reintroducing the Olympic Games was a Greek poet called Panagiotis Soutsos. Greece was now smaller and less successful[55] than many other countries in Europe. Soutsos wanted Greece to be strong and important again. The Olympics, he believed, could help Greece become a great country once more.

Evangelis Zappas

People in Europe were not really interested in athletics at that time and there were no athletics competitions, but a very rich Greek called Evangelis Zappas liked Soutsos's idea. In 1856 he wrote to King Otto of Greece. He wanted King Otto to start the Olympic Games again in Athens. Zappas also wanted to pay for them. Because of this, the Greek government[56] promised to hold an Olympics in 1859. They planned to have lots of competitions for industry and agriculture, and also for athletics.

However, the athletics part of the 1859 Olympics in Athens was not successful. The Greek government thought that the industrial and agricultural Olympics were more important, so the athletics events only took place in a city square. Most of the athletes had not trained hard and there were no seats for the spectators. The people watching the event just stood in the square and most of them could not see anything. But Evangelis Zappas still believed in the idea of the Olympics. When he died a few years later, in 1865, he gave all his money to pay for the modern Olympics.

William Penny Brookes

More than 2,000 kilometres away, in a small village called Much Wenlock in Shropshire, England, a doctor called William Penny Brookes was also becoming very interested in the Olympic Games. He already held a small village games in Much Wenlock every year because he wanted to help villagers become healthier. In the autumn of 1858, Doctor Brookes read about plans for the 1859 Greek Olympics in Athens. He sent money to Athens to buy a prize for one of the winners. He also made his village games bigger and called them the Wenlock Olympian Games. These games are still held every year in the village of Much Wenlock.

In 1866 Doctor Brookes organized England's first National Olympic Games in London. These Games were very successful, with ten thousand spectators, but not everyone liked them. Some rich, important men in England thought it was wrong that the Games were open to everyone, even poor people. They made it difficult for Games like the ones in 1866 to happen again in England.

Meanwhile in Greece the next Zappas Olympics were held in 1870 in the ancient Panathenaic Stadium, which was rebuilt with some of Zappas's money. These Zappas Olympics were very successful. Athletes from every part of Greece competed and thirty thousand spectators watched. Another Zappas Olympics was held in 1875, but this time the organizing committee said that only university students could compete. These Games did not go well, so national Olympics in Greece, just like the Olympics in England, came to an end.

Pierre de Coubertin

Now another man became interested in the idea of a modern Olympic Games. He was a French aristocrat called Pierre de Coubertin. He liked horse-riding, fencing, rowing and boxing and he believed that sport could make people stronger and more successful. He was also very interested in the ancient Olympics and read everything he could find about them. At the same time in England, Doctor Brookes now wanted a modern international Olympic Games. He wrote about it in newspapers and in letters to important people, but nobody was interested. In 1890 Coubertin visited Brookes in Much Wenlock. He decided that he wanted to start a national Olympic Games in France.

In 1892 Coubertin, like Brookes, began to talk about a modern international Olympic Games. He believed that a sports competition between people from different countries could help bring peace to the world. In June 1894, Coubertin organized an International Athletics Congress at the Sorbonne University in Paris. Seventy-nine people from nine different countries came to the meeting, which was held in a room full of pictures from Ancient Greek times. Coubertin wanted the pictures to make people think about the wonderful history of the ancient Olympics.

For the first time, people began to listen to these ideas about a modern Olympic Games. At last, they were interested. The people at the meeting agreed to hold an international Olympic Games in Athens in 1896. They also planned to have an Olympic Games every four years after that, in a different country each time. The International Olympic Committee (IOC) was created and the Greek writer Demetrious Vikelas became its first president.

Pierre de Coubertin

Georgios Averoff

The Greek government agreed to host the first international Olympics. The Greeks then worked very hard to get their country ready for the Games. The Panathenaic stadium in Athens was renovated[57] with money from Zappas and from a very rich Greek architect[58] called Georgios Averoff. Averoff gave more than $100,000 for the work.

The first IOC Olympic Games began on 6th April 1896. Nearly three hundred athletes from fourteen different countries competed in forty-three events. There were nine different sports: athletics, cycling, fencing, gymnastics, shooting, swimming, tennis, weightlifting and wrestling. The swimming races were held in the sea and competitors had to jump out of boats and swim to the shore[59] in ice-cold water. The athletes were all men – women could only watch. The weather was terrible, but the Games were very successful. There were more spectators at the 1896 Olympics than at any sporting event before. An American called James Connolly was the first medal winner of the modern Games. His boat journey from New York to Athens took seventeen days and he spent nearly all his money on his ticket, but he won the 'hop, step and jump' event (now called the triple jump).

The Americans won most of the events in the stadium but the Greek spectators wanted a medal for their country. The last event was a special event called the marathon. Many of the athletics events in the 1896 Olympics were old ones from the ancient Olympics. The marathon was a new event. The idea for it came from a very old story from the second century AD by the Greek writer Lucian. Lucian's story was about a famous battle, or fight, at Marathon, in Greece, in 490 BC. Here, ten thousand Greek troops[60] fought and won against a much larger army from Persia. In the story, a man called Philippides ran from Marathon to Athens, about 40 kilometres away, to tell people about the battle. When he arrived he said, 'We have won!' and then fell down dead. Robert Browning had written a poem in 1879 which made this story famous. At the 1896 Olympics, the new marathon race was 40 kilometres long – the same distance Philippides ran.

For the 1896 marathon, the competitors had to run the 40 kilometres from Marathon to Athens, finishing in the Olympic stadium. The first person to run into the stadium was a Greek competitor, called Spyros Louis. The thousands of spectators in and around the stadium were amazed. Louis won the marathon by more than seven minutes, making everyone in Greece very happy.

The first 'official' modern Olympic Games of 1896 were very successful. It is sad that Doctor Brookes died just four months before they started, but he and Soutsos, Zappas and Coubertin helped bring the Olympics back. After 1896, the Games became the most important sporting event in the world.

5

The Games Grow

The next few years were difficult for the Olympic Games. Because the 1896 Games were so successful, many people wanted the Olympics to stay in Athens. They wanted the Games to be held in Greece every time, but the IOC wanted different host countries for every Olympics.

The next Games, in 1900, were held in Paris, at the same time as the Paris World's Fair[61], but they were not a success. The organizers of the Fair did not work with the IOC, there was no stadium and there were not many spectators. The events were held over five months and many people did not even know that these events were part of the Olympic Games.

The same thing happened in 1904, when the Games were held in the USA during the St Louis World's Fair. Nearly all the athletes were North American and the Games were badly organized. The marathon was probably the most badly organized event of all. The roads were hot and covered with dirt. Horses and cars went in front of the runners, so they made the roads even dirtier. One competitor decided he could not run any further, so he walked back to the stadium to get his belongings. When the judges saw him, they thought he was the first marathon runner to finish the race. They gave him a medal but he only ran 14.5 kilometres!

Pierre de Coubertin did not go to the St Louis Olympics and teams from many of the countries who were at the 1896 Games stayed at home, too. Two new events – boxing and freestyle wrestling – were added at St Louis, but everyone was so busy with the World's Fair that the Olympic Games were almost forgotten.

Were the modern Olympic Games going to die out[62] after just three Games? It certainly seemed possible. Then the Games came back to Greece once more, for an 'extra' games between the official ones organized by the IOC. So in 1906 the Greeks held their second modern Olympics. At last the Games started to move forward again. The 1906 Olympics were bigger and better than the 1896 Games and people began to feel excited about them once more. The 1906 Games probably stopped the Olympics from dying out, but the IOC still say that they were unofficial.

After 1906 the Games began to grow and their future started to feel safe. The 1908 Games were held in Great Britain, in London. These Games were well organized and many of the events took place in a special new stadium. In 1912 Stockholm in Sweden hosted the Games. The 1912 Games became known as the 'Jim Thorpe Olympics' because of one athlete's incredible achievements[63]. Jim Thorpe won a gold medal in both the pentathlon (an event with five different sports) and the decathlon (an event with ten different sports). He became famous around the world and because of his success people were more interested in the Olympics. The Stockholm Games were so well organized that for many years after them the Olympics were run in the same way as the Stockholm Games.

By 1924, when the Games were held in Paris, France, teams from forty-four different countries were competing. At last the Olympics were a great international event, and in the next years they grew more and more. There were more spectators, more countries competing, more sports and more events. Basketball and canoeing events began in 1936, and judo and volleyball began in 1964. By 1952, in Helsinki, there were 149 events in 17 different sports; by 2004, in Athens, there were 301 events in 28 sports. Even today, new sports are still being added. In 2008 a marathon 10 kilometre swimming race was held for the first time and BMX cycling also became a new Olympic sport.

At almost every Olympics, new changes have been made, slowly turning the Games into the event we know today. In 1904 gold, silver and bronze medals were given for the first time to the athletes who came first, second and third in their events. In 1906 there was another change: athletes were sent to the Olympics by their national Olympic committee and came as part of a team. At these Games, too, the parade of nations was introduced at the opening ceremony: athletes from each country walked around the stadium in groups so that all the spectators could see them.

For the first sixty years of the modern Olympics, the parade at the closing ceremony was also organized in this way, but in 1956, for the Melbourne Games in Australia, a boy called John Wing wrote to the organizers with a new idea. He thought that at the closing ceremony, athletes should come into the stadium all together, to show world unity. The organizers liked his idea and made the change for the 1956 Games and all the Games from then on. When the Olympics came back to Australia in 2000, the organizers found John Wing, an old man by then. They invited him to watch the closing ceremony at which athletes still come in together as a result of his idea.

The London Games of 1908 made a small but interesting change to the marathon event. Because the British king and queen wanted to watch the start of the event from their castle in Windsor, the race was made longer, to 42.195 kilometres. Every marathon since then has been exactly 42.195 kilometres long!

At Stockholm in 1912 automatic timing devices[64] and the photo-finish camera were used for the first time for track events. When two competitors finish a race at almost exactly the same moment, the photo finish can help the judges decide who the winner is. At the 1912 Games they also introduced a public-address system[65], so that the organizers could give information about the events and winners to the spectators.

The Olympic flag was first used in 1920 at the Antwerp Games, in Belgium, and also in 1920 the Athletes' Oath – or promise – was included in the opening ceremony, too. For the Oath, a specially chosen athlete promises that the competitors will take part fairly for their country and for the greatness of their sport. The first athlete to do this was the Belgian athlete Victor Boin, who held the Olympic flag and made this Oath for everyone at the Antwerp Games in 1920.

An important change came in 1924 when the first Winter Olympic Games were held in Chamonix, France. At these Games there were skiing, figure skating and ice hockey. The Winter Olympics were held in the same year as the Summer Games until 1992, but they are now held in the middle of each Olympiad, two years after the Summer Games. It is not easy to become a very good skier or skater if you live in a hot country that has no mountains! Because of this, a smaller number of countries enter the Winter Olympics compared with the Summer Olympics. The Winter Games are now much bigger than they were in 1924. In the 2002 Winter Olympics in Salt Lake City in the USA, nearly 2,400 athletes competed in 78 events.

Skier Bode Miller of the USA competing at the 2002 Salt Lake City Winter Olympic Games

Another very important year for the Olympics was 1928, when the Games were held in Amsterdam, in the Netherlands. Here, for the first time, women were allowed to compete in gymnastics, track and field (jumping and throwing) events. There were no women athletes at the first modern Olympic Games of 1896, and in 1900 women were only allowed to compete in 'gentle' games like tennis and croquet. With so many new events now open to women, the number of athletes competing in the Amsterdam Games was double[66] that of 1924. At the end of the women's 800 metre final, some of the competitors needed help from a doctor. When the president of the IOC, Henri de Baillot-Latour of Belgium, saw this, he said that all women's Olympics sports should be stopped. Other members of the IOC did not agree with him, but there were no more women's races longer than 200 metres until 1956.

There was another change made for the first time at the 1928 Amsterdam Games. This was a change in the parade of nations at the opening ceremony. For the first time, the Greek team walked at the front of the parade and the host team at the back.

In 1932, in Los Angeles, USA, the medal ceremony was changed. Medal winners now stood on a podium – a special high step – while the flag of their country was raised. At the Los Angeles Games, athletes stayed in an Olympic village for the first time.

Between 1900 and 1928, the Summer Olympics always ran for more than eleven weeks. But after the Los Angeles Games, the Summer Olympics became shorter. This brought a big change to the Games. The 1932 Los Angeles Olympics were only sixteen days long and since 1932 the Summer Games have only ever been between fifteen and eighteen days long.

Another important tradition began four years later, at the 1936 Berlin Olympics. For these Games, a lighted torch was taken from Olympia in Greece to the Berlin stadium by 3,422 people. In a special relay, each person ran carrying the torch for one kilometre before giving it to the next person. Since then, the torch relay has begun every Olympic Games, just as the sacred truce once started the ancient Games. The Olympic torch has been carried by foot, aeroplane, road, train and boat. For the 2000 Sydney Games in Australia, divers even carried a special torch under the water. And in 2008 the torch was taken up Mount Everest, the highest mountain in the world.

Countries choose special people to bring the torch into the stadium. At the 1988 Games in Seoul, South Korea, a famous South Korean athlete, Sohn Kee-chung, brought the torch into the stadium. He was seventy-six years old. He was the winner of the 1936 Olympic marathon.

The Olympic torch relay in Beijing, 2008

The 1936 Games were special because they were shown on television for the first time. Very few people had televisions in their homes at this time, but twenty-five large screens[67] were put up in Berlin so that people could watch the Games for free. It was only in 1948 that the London Olympics were shown on home television for the first time, but even then not many people had televisions in their homes.

Since that time, of course, television and computers have become important around the world. Because it is easier to travel and to find out about what is happening in other parts of the world, more and more people now watch and compete in the Olympics. Four billion[68] people watched the Beijing Olympics of 2008 – that's more than half the people in the world!

6

Olympic Sports and Great Olympians

Today, there are around thirty different sports and more than three hundred events at the Olympic Games. At every Olympics, new names become famous. Athletes surprise spectators by winning or losing. Some take home several medals and some set incredible new world records. Others show that they are great Olympians because of their bravery[69] or kindness.

Track events

Some of the most exciting events at the Olympics are the track events. Track events are races that take place or finish on the track in the Olympic stadium. Some of these races are among the oldest events of the Olympics. Running races were the first events of the ancient Olympics and athletes have competed in the 100 metre, 400 metre and 1500 metre races since the first modern Games in Athens in 1896. Today there are other track events as well, like the 200 metre and 10,000 metre races, and the 20,000 metre walk. There are also team relays and hurdle events – races in which athletes run and jump over small fences.

In the years since the first modern 100 metre race, runners have become faster and faster. In 1896 the record for the 100 metres was 12 seconds, but in 2008 Usain Bolt ran it in only 9.69 seconds. One of the greatest Olympic runners in history, Jesse Owens, took home four gold medals from the 1936 Games. He won the 100 metres, 200 metres and 4 × 100 metre relay, and also the long jump. In 1984 the American athlete Carl Lewis won the same events as Jesse Owens almost fifty years before. Another runner who won several gold medals in track events was Paavo Nurmi from Finland, also called the Flying Finn. At the 1920, 1924 and 1928 Olympics, he won nine gold and three silver medals in long-distance[70] races.

One famous female runner was the Dutch athlete Fanny Blankers-Koen. She was thirty years old and the mother of two children when in 1948 she won gold in the women's 100 metres, 200 metres, 80 metre hurdles and 4 × 100 metre relay.

Field events

The field events include sports in which the athletes have to jump and throw. Like most track events, field events are also held in the stadium. Some of these events have been part of the Olympics for many years, but most have changed a lot since they first began. In the pole vault, athletes use a pole, or long stick, to jump over a high bar. At the first modern Olympics in 1896, pole vaulters used heavy wooden poles and the world record was only 3.3 metres. Now, vaulting poles are made of the light, modern material fibreglass[71]. In 1985, using one of these poles, an athlete jumped higher than six metres for the first time.

Pole vaulters' poles are easier to use now, but modern javelins are actually more difficult to throw. In 1986 javelins were changed because athletes were throwing them too far. People thought the sport was becoming too dangerous because a javelin might hit a spectator or another athlete. In 1984 Uwe Hohn from Germany threw a javelin 104.8 metres, but with the new kind of javelin, the world record is 98.48 metres.

One of the greatest field athletes was Bob Beamon of the USA. He jumped an incredible 8.9 metres in the long jump in 1968. His jump broke the old record by 55 centimetres and his new record lasted for more than twenty years.

Jim Thorpe is famous for his achievements in field and track athletics at the 1912 Olympics. At these Games, Thorpe won a gold medal for the modern pentathlon. This was an event from the ancient Olympics in which athletes took part in five sports. For the 1912 pentathlon, athletes competed in the long jump, javelin and discus, and in the 200 metre and 1500 metre races. After the pentathlon, Thorpe also came fourth in the high jump and seventh in the long jump. He then broke the world record in the decathlon, winning another gold medal.

Today the pentathlon has changed again and is now a group of five different sports – shooting, fencing, swimming, horse-riding and running. Many great athletes still take part in the decathlon. For this they must run 100 metres, 400 metres and 1500 metres. They also have to compete in the 110 metre hurdles, the long and high jumps, the pole vault and three throwing events. For women, there is the heptathlon – a group of seven running, jumping and throwing events.

Gymnastics

Gymnastics are another of the oldest Olympic sports. They were popular in Ancient Greece and there have been gymnastics events at the modern Olympics since 1896. In gymnastics, there are no races to win. Gymnasts compete in front of a group of judges, who give them a score[72], taking away points for every mistake. Until 1976 the judges had never given a gymnast a perfect score but in that year's Olympic Games in Montreal,

Canada, fourteen-year-old Nadia Comăneci of Romania was awarded a perfect score for the first time. Not surprisingly, Nadia Comăneci won three gold medals, one silver and one bronze at these Olympics.

Fourteen-year-old Nadia Comăneci competing at the 1976 Montreal Games

Another great gymnast was the Russian Alexander Dityatin. In the 1980 Olympics, Dityatin won a medal in *every* men's gymnastics event. With three gold medals, four silver and one bronze, he became the first athlete to win eight medals at one Olympics.

Water sports

Swimming and diving are perhaps the best-known Olympic water sports. There are also boat races like canoeing, rowing and sailing, and water polo, a team game played in a swimming pool. One of the most famous Olympic swimmers was the American Johnny Weissmuller. He was the first man to swim 100 metres in less than a minute and he won five Olympic gold medals. In later years he also became a famous actor and played Tarzan in twelve films. Another American swimmer, Michael Phelps, has broken many records. At the 2008 Beijing Games, he won eight gold medals, setting a new record for the most gold medals won in one Olympic Games.

Swimmer Michael Phelps competing in the 400 metre race

The British rower Steve Redgrave quickly became famous for winning gold medals in five Olympic Games, but it took more time for people to remember the canoeist Birgit Fischer's name. She won her first gold medal in 1980 when she was only eighteen years old and she won her eighth gold medal twenty-four years later in 2004!

New Olympic sports

As well as more traditional sports like boxing, wrestling and weightlifting, many new events have been added to the Olympics over the years. There were no team sports at the ancient Olympics, but now there are team events in baseball, basketball, football, handball, hockey, softball and volleyball. Badminton, table tennis and tennis are also played and there are equestrian (horse-riding) and cycling events. There are less well-known Olympic sports too, like archery, shooting, fencing, judo and taekwondo. For athletes who are good at different sports, there is also the triathlon. This includes three events – swimming, cycling and running races.

Winter sports

At the Winter Olympics, there are events in snow and ice sports like ice-skating, skiing and bobsledding. Usually different athletes compete in the Winter and Summer Games, but in 1988 Christa Luding-Rothenburger of East Germany won medals in both. She took gold and silver medals in ice-skating at the Winter Olympics in Calgary and then won a silver medal in a cycling event at the Summer Olympics in Seoul in the same year.

Other great Olympians

The youngest Olympian ever was Dimitrios Loundras of Greece. He won a bronze medal in gymnastics in 1896, when he was just ten years old. Aged seventy-two, Oscar Swahn of

Sweden was the oldest athlete to take part in the Olympics. He became the oldest person to win an Olympic medal when he came second in a shooting event at the 1920 Olympics.

Many Olympic athletes have become famous not only for the medals they have won but also for their bravery. The American gymnast George Eyser won three gold medals, two silvers and one bronze at the 1904 St Louis Games. This was a great achievement for any man, but for Eyser it was incredible. He was an amputee[73] and competed at the Olympics with a wooden leg.

Károly Takács of Hungary was hoping to compete in the shooting event at the Tokyo Olympics planned for 1940, but in 1938 Takács was hurt in an accident, and he could no longer use the hand he normally shot with. The Tokyo Olympics were cancelled[74] because of the Second World War, but Takács learnt to shoot with his left hand and won an Olympic gold medal in 1948.

Konrad von Wangenheim of Germany also showed his bravery. At the 1936 Olympics, during one of the equestrian events, he fell from his horse and broke his collarbone[75]. Because he did not want his team to lose, he got back on his horse and finished the event. He was badly hurt, but he also rode the next day and this helped the German team to win a gold medal.

The American Ray Ewry was another brave Olympian who fought off health problems to win at the Olympics. When he was a boy he became very ill. He could not walk and had to stay in a wheelchair[76], but he decided to teach himself to walk again. Incredibly, he learnt to walk and then he started to jump too. Between 1900 and 1908 he won eight gold medals in jumping events at the Olympics.

These athletes are remembered today for their bravery and their great achievements. Some Olympians, like the weightlifter Charles Vinci, are remembered for funnier things.

Weightlifters cannot compete if they are too heavy. In 1956 Vinci was told fifteen minutes before his event that he was 200 grams too heavy. So Vinci cut all his hair off and was then allowed to take part. He won a gold medal and set a world record after his haircut!

7

Events in History

Since the modern Games began, more than a hundred years ago, events in history have often changed what happens at the Olympics. Sometimes, the Olympics have also changed what happens in history!

The only events which stopped the Olympics were the two world wars of 1914–1918 and 1939–1945. In 1916 the Olympics were cancelled for the first time, and Antwerp in Belgium was chosen as the host country for the 1920 Games. The Belgian people had a terrible time during the war and the IOC wanted to give them something back. Germany, Austria, Hungary, Bulgaria and Turkey were not allowed to compete because they had attacked other countries during the war.

It was difficult to buy building materials after the war, so when the 1920 Antwerp Olympics began, the stadium was still unfinished. People did not have much money, so there were fewer spectators than at most Games.

The 1932 Los Angeles Olympics had the same problem. These Games were held in the middle of the Great Depression – a difficult period when many people lost their jobs and all their money. Because of this, at first many people did not buy tickets. Then some famous celebrities[77], including Charlie Chaplin, promised to entertain[78] the spectators and people began to buy tickets. But the Games were not very successful. There were only 1,300 athletes at the Games (compared with nearly 2,900 at the 1928 Games) and the football event was cancelled completely.

The 1936 Games came at a difficult time in history. Berlin was the chosen host city for these Olympics, but by 1936 Hitler's Nazis[79] were ruling Germany. The Nazis only wanted blonde-haired, blue-eyed Aryan people to live in Germany. The Nazis wanted Jewish[80] people and other groups of people to leave the country. Hitler believed that Aryan people were stronger and faster than everybody else. He wanted everyone to see this at the Berlin Olympic Games and he was very angry when the black African-American athlete Jesse Owens won four gold medals.

Jesse Owens competing at the 1936 Berlin Games

Japan was going to host the 1940 Olympics. When Japan attacked China in 1937, the IOC asked Finland to be the host country. Then, in 1939, the Second World War began and the Games were cancelled for the second time in their history. Because of the war, there were also no Games in 1944. Since 1948 there have always been Summer Olympics every four years.

The first Games after the war, in 1948, were held in London. Many parts of London were destroyed during the war, so the city was still being rebuilt in 1948. There was very little money for the Games. A new stadium was not built, and athletes had to bring their own food and sleep in army camps[81] and schools. Japan and Germany, who attacked other countries during the war, were not invited. At first, many people did not want to hold the Olympic Games so soon after the Second World War, but the 1948 Games were very successful and over four thousand athletes from fifty-nine countries came.

Fanny Blankers-Koen winning the 100 metres at the 1948 London Games

In the 1950s, some countries began to boycott[82] the Olympic Games – they stayed away and did not compete. They did this to show that they were angry about things that were happening in the world. The first big Olympic boycotts were in 1956 at the Melbourne Olympics. Egypt, Iraq and Lebanon stayed away because they were angry about Israel's invasion[83] of parts of Egypt. The Netherlands, Spain and Switzerland also boycotted the 1956 Games because of the Soviet[84] invasion of Hungary.

The biggest Olympic boycott was in 1980, when the host city was Moscow, in the Soviet Union. Because of the Soviet Union's invasion of Afghanistan in 1979, President Jimmy Carter of the USA asked many countries to boycott the Games. Over sixty countries including the USA did not go to the 1980 Olympics. There were only eighty countries competing – the lowest number since 1956.

In 1984, when the next Olympics came to Los Angeles, the Soviet Union decided to do the same thing. They organized a boycott as Los Angeles is in the USA, and fourteen countries stayed away. Between them, these fourteen countries held more than half of the gold medals from the 1976 Olympics, so they were important competitors.

Countries can decide to boycott the Games, but the IOC also has the power to tell countries that they cannot come to the Games. In the past the government of South Africa had a system of apartheid, which meant that black people were forced to live apart from white people and many people there had very difficult lives just because they were black. Because of this, in 1964, the IOC banned South Africa from the Games. South Africa did not come to the Olympics again until 1992, when the country began to break down apartheid.

Usually, athletes promise to compete fairly in the Olympics and do not bring the problems of their country into the Games, but there are sometimes arguments. At the 1956 Games, just one month after the Soviet Union's invasion of Hungary, the two countries competed against each other in the water polo final. The Soviet and Hungarian teams began to fight each other and the judges had to stop the game.

Forty-five Hungarian athletes also used the 1956 Games to leave their country. They did not want to go back there while there was a Soviet government, so they stayed in Melbourne after the Games.

8

Problems at the Olympics

Pierre de Coubertin once said, 'The most important thing in the Olympic Games is not to win but to take part, just as the most important thing in life is not the triumph[85] but the struggle[86].'

This is what many athletes believe. But some Olympic athletes do not agree and find it very difficult when they lose. In 1972, when the Pakistan hockey team lost in the final, they threw water at the officials[87]!

Other Olympic athletes have wanted to win so badly, for themselves and for their country, that they have cheated[88]. Cheating is as old as the Games themselves. At the 100th Olympic Games, the city of Ephesus wanted to have a champion, so they bribed the winner of the long race, Sotades. Sotades was from the island of Crete, but people from Ephesus paid him to say that he was from their city. When the people of Crete heard about this, Sotades was exiled – he was never allowed to go back to his home island.

In 338 BC, the boxer Eupolus of Thessaly bribed his three competitors – he gave them money to let him win. When the judges heard about this, they made all the men pay a fine[89]. With the money from the fine, they built statues of Zeus. The writing on the statues told everyone that these men were cheats.

This did not stop people cheating. Another cheat of the ancient Games was Callipus of Athens. At the 322 BC Olympics, Callipus also bribed his competitors in the pentathlon to let him win the event. He and the competitors he bribed all had to pay a fine. The judges then used the money to build more statues of Zeus.

The modern Olympics have had similar problems. In 1904, American marathon runner Fred Lorz ran some of the marathon but travelled almost half the way by car. He arrived first and was getting ready to collect his gold medal when he admitted he had travelled in the car. Lorz said he had done this as a joke.

At the 1976 Olympics in Montreal, Boris Onishchenko, a member of the Soviet pentathlon team, used a special sword[90] in the fencing. Fencing swords light up when one competitor hits the other, and the first competitor then wins a point. Onishchenko added a special button to his sword so that it lit up every time he pushed it. He kept winning points, but he had not really touched the other competitor. The Soviet team had a good chance of winning the pentathlon in 1976, but because Onishchenko was disqualified[91], they had to leave the event.

During the 1960s, some competitors began to cheat in other ways. They started to use drugs to help them run or swim faster, jump higher or fight better. In 1968, in Mexico City, the IOC began to test athletes to find out if they were taking drugs. Athletes taking drugs were disqualified. The first person disqualified from the Olympics was Hans-Gunnar Liljenwall in 1968. He failed the test because of a few glasses of beer. He said he drank the beer because he was so worried about shooting in the pentathlon.

One of the most famous people to fail a drugs test was the runner Ben Johnson. He won the 100 metres in Seoul in 1988 and set a new world record, but then he failed a drugs test. Johnson had to give back his medal and he was not allowed to compete in athletics for two years.

One of the most terrible events of the modern Olympics was at the 1972 Munich Games. Eight Palestinian terrorists[92] went into the Olympic village. They were angry that there were many Palestinian people in prison in Israel. The terrorists found the Israeli team and killed two of them. They also took another nine Israelis hostage[93] and said they were going to kill them if people did not do what they asked. The terrorists wanted two hundred Palestinian people who were in prison in Israel to be let out. They also wanted to go home safely from Germany. The German police tried to shoot at the terrorists, but everything went wrong. The nine Israeli hostages, five of the terrorists and one policeman were all killed.

After the shootings, the Munich Games were stopped and there was a memorial service[94] in the stadium. The next day the Games started again. The IOC wanted to show the terrorists that they could not stop the Olympics. When people think of the Munich Olympics of 1972, they usually remember this terrible event more than the many sporting achievements.

There was also terrorism at the Olympics in Atlanta in 1996. A bomb[95] killed one person and hurt more than a hundred others. These were very difficult times in the history of the Olympics, but they are very unusual. The real history of the Olympics is one of bravery, kindness and incredible achievement.

The memorial service at the 1972 Munich Games for the Israeli athletes who were killed by terrorists

9

The Paralympics

Shortly after each Summer and Winter Olympic Games, the Paralympic Games are held. They are called Paralympics because the Greek word *para* means alongside or next to. These Games are for athletes with a disability and are held just 'next to', or after, the Olympics.

The Paralympics first began in the 1940s at Stoke Mandeville Hospital in Aylesbury, England. They were the idea of Ludwig Guttmann, a doctor from Germany who lived in England. At that time there were many people with injuries[96] from the Second World War. Guttmann believed that sports could be very helpful for these people. In 1948, while the London Olympics were going on, Guttmann organized the Stoke Mandeville Games for athletes in wheelchairs. For these Games, two British teams of men and women who had fought in the war competed in archery in the gardens of Stoke Mandeville Hospital. The Games were held every year after that and in 1952, when a Dutch team also competed, they became the International Stoke Mandeville Games.

Guttmann wanted an international sports competition for people with disabilities to be held every four years, just like the Olympic Games. This happened twelve years after the first Stoke Mandeville Games, when Rome in Italy hosted the 1960 International Stoke Mandeville Games. Four hundred wheelchair athletes from twenty-three countries competed in the first Paralympics in Rome and the event was a great success. The only big problem was that the Olympic village was not built for wheelchairs, so people had to carry the athletes up and down stairs.

From then on, the Paralympics grew very quickly. In

Toronto in 1976 there were 1,657 competitors, and there were new events for different disability groups: amputees and visually impaired[97] athletes came to the Games for the first time. Special racing wheelchairs were also introduced at these Games. At the 1980 Arnhem Paralympics in the Netherlands, events for athletes with cerebral palsy[98] also began.

An athlete competing at the 1992 Barcelona Paralympics

The Paralympics have always been held in the same year as the Olympic Games and at Seoul in 1988 they were held for the first time in the same host city. The host city that is chosen to host the Olympic Games also now agrees to host the Paralympics.

In 1976 the first Winter Paralympics were held in Örnsköldsvik in Sweden. At these Games, teams from sixteen countries competed in skiing events. By 2010, at the Winter

Paralympics in Vancouver, Canada, around five hundred athletes from forty-four nations took part.

The Paralympics are now the second biggest sporting event in the world, after the Olympics themselves. There are twenty-two summer sports and five winter sports at the Paralympics, with events for six different groups of athletes with disabilities. Athletes with cerebral palsy, wheelchair users, visually impaired athletes, amputees, athletes with other physical disabilities and athletes with intellectual[99] disabilities all compete at the Paralympics in sports from skiing to gymnastics. The event has become very important in the newspapers and on television. The number of people who watched the 2010 Vancouver Winter Paralympics on television was 1.6 billion.

One of the greatest Paralympians is the swimmer Trischa Zorn. She competed at seven Paralympic Games between 1980 and 2004, and won fifty-five medals (including forty-one gold medals) in the events for visually impaired athletes.

The Danish wheelchair athlete Connie Hansen won five events at the 1988 Paralympic Games in Seoul. She took home gold medals for the 400 metre, 800 metre, 1500 metre and 5,000 metre races and for the wheelchair marathon. She also won the wheelchair marathon again at the 1992 Games in Barcelona.

Tanni Grey-Thompson of Great Britain is another incredible wheelchair athlete. She was the first woman to finish the 400 metre race in less than a minute. She won four gold medals at the 1992 Barcelona Paralympics, four more in Sydney in 2000 and another two in Athens in 2004.

Roberto Marson of Italy is a Paralympian in more than one sport. At the 1968 Paralympics he won three gold medals in field athletics, three more in swimming and four in wheelchair fencing.

Ludwig Guttmann always believed that competing in sport can bring people with disabilities better health, a feeling of achievement, and friendship. Today, hundreds of athletes compete in the Paralympics, and millions of people around the world enjoy watching.

Athletes competing in wheelchair basketball at the 2008 Beijing Paralympics

10

Today and into the Future

The Olympic Games have changed a lot since the first modern Games of 1896 and they are still changing today.

With more athletes than ever competing in a record number of events, it is becoming more and more expensive to host the Olympics – in 2008 China spent more than $40 billion on the Beijing Games! Providing accommodation and transport are huge costs for the host country. Millions of spectators now come to watch their countries' teams compete and to visit the host country. At Beijing, about seven million spectator tickets were sold. Before each Games, the host country has to organize the accommodation and transport for the spectators and athletes. Because some of the events are held at different places in and around the host city, public transport has to work very well.

The host country's organizing committee also has to spend a lot of money on security – policemen and others who keep the athletes and spectators safe. In Athens in 2004, this cost around $800 million.

The 1976 Games in Montreal were so expensive that the Montreal government only finished paying for them thirty years later. People could see that the Olympics were becoming too expensive so for the 1984 Los Angeles Games, corporate sponsors were used for the first time. These were companies who paid money to the organizing committee for publicity[100]. Their name or logo was then shown on every piece of information about the Games. Because corporate sponsors paid so much money, the Los Angeles Olympics actually made more money than was spent. Since 1984, corporate sponsors have always been used at the Olympics. In 1996 companies paid $200 million to sponsor the Atlanta Games in the USA.

Security during the Olympic torch relay in San Francisco, 2008

The Olympic organizing committees now also make money from selling television rights[101]. Many television companies want to be able to show the Olympics and they pay a lot of money for this. Television companies paid $1.5 billion for the rights to show the 2004 Athens Games.

When the modern Olympics first started, no one had televisions or computers, but now communications[102] are getting better every year. In 2012, it is thought that up to four billion people will watch the London Olympics on the television or Internet, or read about them in newspapers. Reports about the London Olympics will be sent out from an International Broadcast Centre by twenty thousand broadcasters[103], photographers and journalists.

Communications are not the only technology[104] that is changing with every Olympiad. Electronic timing devices and photo-finish equipment can now decide the winner of almost every race. This was very useful at the Sydney Games in 2000, when two competitors, Haile Gebrselassie and Paul Tergat, finished a race at almost exactly the same time. The photo-finish and timing devices were able to show that Gebrselassie was the winner of the 10,000 metre race by only 0.09 seconds!

The Olympic motto[105] is the Latin phrase *Citius, Altius, Fortius* (meaning 'Faster, Higher, Stronger'). At each Olympic Games, every athlete tries to be better than all the others and new world records are set.

Who will be the greatest athletes at the next Olympic Games? The 2012 Games are in London, Great Britain, and this makes London the only city that has hosted the Olympics three times. The 2016 Games are in Rio de Janeiro, Brazil. Some athletes will go home with no medals, others will become famous in their countries and around the world. What we do know is that there will be some incredible races, jumps, throws and games.

The ancient Olympics went on for more than a thousand years. The modern Olympics are only a little more than a hundred years old, but they are the most important athletic competition in the world. Perhaps one day people will celebrate a thousand years of the modern Olympics!

Points for Understanding

1

1 How often are the Summer Olympics held?
2 What medal does an athlete win if he or she comes in second place?
3 Who organizes the Olympic Games?
4 What does the Olympic flag look like?
5 What happens in Olympia in Greece several months before each Olympic Games?
6 Who is always at the front of the parade of athletes at the Olympic opening ceremony, and why?
7 Why are pigeons released at the opening ceremony?

2

1 Why was Greece so important in the world when the Olympics first started? Give two reasons.
2 When were the first Olympic Games that were written about?
3 What was the only event at the first Olympic Games?
4 What was the name of the time of peace before every ancient Olympic Games?
5 What happened to married women who went to watch the ancient Olympic Games?

3

1 Why did more people come to the Olympic Games after 456 BC?
2 What were the main sports events at the Olympic Games by 400 BC?
3 What were the two things competitors could not do in the *pankration*?
4 What were the prizes for winners at the early Olympic Games?
5 When were the ancient Olympic Games stopped?

4

1 Name the five important people who helped to start the modern Olympics.
2 When were the first international Olympic Games held?
3 Why was the marathon 40 kilometres long?
4 Why was the marathon at the first Olympics so exciting for the Greek spectators?

5

1 Why were the 1900 and 1904 Olympic Games not successful?
2 Where were the 1908 Olympic Games held?
3 When was the parade of nations introduced at the opening ceremony?
4 Why was John Wing invited to watch the closing ceremony of the Sydney Olympics in 2000?
5 Why did the marathon become 42.195 kilometres long in 1908?
6 When and where were the first Winter Olympic Games held?
7 Why were the 1928 Olympics so important for women?

6

1 What are Olympic track events?
2 How many gold medals did the Flying Finn win?
3 Why were javelins changed in 1986?
4 What events did Jim Thorpe win gold medals for at the 1912 Olympics?
5 What events make up today's modern pentathlon?
6 What did Nadia Comăneci do for the first time in Olympic history in 1976?
7 Who won five Olympic gold medals and also played Tarzan in twelve films?
8 Name three Winter Olympic sports.
9 How did Konrad von Wangenheim show his bravery at the 1936 Olympics?

7

1 When and why were the Olympic Games cancelled?
2 Why were there only 1,300 athletes at the 1932 Los Angeles Olympics?
3 What is an Olympic boycott?
4 Why did sixty-five countries boycott the 1980 Moscow Olympics?
5 When was South Africa banned from the Olympics, and why?

8

1 How did Fred Lorz cheat in the 1904 Olympic marathon?
2 Why did the Soviet team leave the pentathlon at the 1976 Olympics?
3 What happened to Ben Johnson after he won the 100 metre race at Seoul in 1988?
4 How many people died during the terrorist attack at the Munich Olympics in 1972?

9

1 Why did Ludwig Guttmann start the Stoke Mandeville Games?
2 When and where were the first international Paralympics held?
3 How many sports are there at the Paralympics?
4 How many Paralympic medals did Trischa Zorn win between 1980 and 2004?

10

1. What are some of the biggest costs for Olympic organizing committees?
2. In what two ways do organizing committees now make money for the Olympics?
3. Why were photo-finish equipment and electronic timing devices needed to decide the winner of the 10,000 metres in the year 2000?
4. What is the Olympic motto, and what does it mean?

Glossary

1 ***athlete*** (page 8)
someone who is good at sports and takes part in sports competitions. An *athletic* person is physically strong and good at sports.

2 ***spectator*** (page 8)
someone who watches a public activity or event

3 ***stadium*** (page 8)
a large building, usually without a roof, where people watch sports events such as races or football matches

4 ***fairly*** (page 8)
in a way that is honest and follows the rules

5 ***fireworks*** (page 8)
objects that make loud noises and coloured lights in the sky when they explode

6 ***event*** (page 8)
an organized occasion such as a sports competition or party

7 ***compete*** – *to compete (in something)* (page 8)
to try to win a *competition* – an organized event in which people try to win medals or prizes by being better than other people

8 ***race*** (page 8)
a competition that decides who is the fastest at doing something

9 ***medal*** (page 8)
a small flat piece of metal that you are given for winning a competition or for doing something that is very brave

10 ***disability*** (page 8)
a condition in which someone is not able to use a part of their body normally

11 ***team*** (page 8)
a group of people who play a sport or game against another group

12 ***organized*** – *to organize something* (page 9)
to prepare or arrange an activity or event

13 ***committee*** (page 9)
a group of people who represent a larger group or organization and are chosen to do a particular job

14 ***torch*** (page 9)
a beautiful piece of metal with a flame at one end that is used to light the fire that burns at the Olympics

15 ***ceremony*** (page 10)
a formal event with lots of people and special traditions, actions or words

16 ***parade*** (page 11)
the part of the ceremony when all the athletes who are competing at the event walk through the stadium past all the spectators

17 ***speech*** (page 11)
a formal occasion when someone speaks to an audience, or the words that someone speaks to an audience

18 ***cauldron*** (page 11)
a large metal container that contains the fire that burns at the Olympics

19 ***pigeon*** (page 11)
a white bird. Pigeons can also be brown or grey and often live in cities.

20 ***peace*** (page 11)
a situation in which there is no war between countries or groups

21 ***judge*** (page 11)
someone who decides who the winner of a competition will be

22 ***disappointment*** (page 11)
the feeling of being unhappy because something did not happen or because someone or something was not as good as you expected

23 **BC** – *before Christ* (page 13)
used after a date to show that it refers to a time before the birth of Jesus Christ. We use AD (*anno Domini*) before a date to show that it is later than the birth of Jesus Christ.

24 ***the Mediterranean*** (page 13)
the countries that surround the Mediterranean Sea – the sea that has Europe to the north and North Africa to the south

25 ***ruled*** – *to rule* (page 13)
to officially control a country or area

26 ***god*** (page 13)
one of the male spirits with special powers that some people believe in and worship. A female spirit like this is called a *goddess*.

27 ***religious*** (page 13)
relating to *religion* – belief in a god or in gods, or a particular system of beliefs in a god or gods

28 ***funeral*** (page 13)
a ceremony that takes place after someone dies

29 ***chariot*** (page 13)
a vehicle with two wheels and no roof that was pulled by horses in races and battles in ancient times

30 ***olive*** (page 14)
a small black or green fruit that is eaten or used for its oil

31 ***modern*** (page 15)
relating to or belonging to recent times or the present

32 ***ancient*** (page 15)
relating to a period of history a very long time ago. Ancient Greece refers to Greece in the period from the eighth century BC to the year 146 BC, when Greece became part of the Roman Empire.

33 ***slave*** (page 15)
someone who belongs by law to another person and who has to obey them and work for them

34 ***allowed*** – *to allow someone to do something* (page 15)
to give someone permission to do something or have something

35 ***take part*** – *to take part (in something)* (page 15)
to be involved in an activity with other people

36 ***train*** – *to train* (page 15)
to practise a sport regularly before a match or competition

37 ***naked*** (page 15)
not wearing any clothes

38 ***temple*** (page 16)
a building that is used for worship in some religions

39 ***statue*** (page 16)
an image made of stone. A statue can also be of a person or animal, and made of wood, metal, etc.

40 ***sand*** (page 18)
a pale brown substance that you find at a beach or in the desert, formed from very small pieces of rock

41 ***bite*** – *to bite someone or something* (page 19)
to use your teeth to hurt someone. *To bite something* usually means to cut or break it in order to eat it.

42 ***poke out*** – *to poke something out* (page 19)
to remove something by pushing it quickly with your finger or a pointed object

43 ***century*** (page 19)
a period of a hundred years, usually counted from a year ending in -00

44 ***crown*** (page 19)
a circular decoration that someone wears on their head

45 ***branch*** (page 19)
a part of a tree that grows out of the tree's trunk, or main stem. The olive branches had leaves on them.

46 ***celebration*** (page 19)
a party or special event at which you *celebrate* something – do something enjoyable in order to show that an occasion or event is special

47 ***Christianity*** (page 20)
the religion that is based on the ideas of Jesus Christ

48 ***Emperor*** (page 20)
a man who rules an *empire* – a number of countries that are ruled by one person or government

49 ***destroyed*** – *to destroy something* (page 20)
to damage something so severely that it cannot exist as it was before

50 ***ruins*** (page 20)
the parts of a building that remain after it has fallen down or been severely damaged

51 ***earthquake*** (page 20)
a sudden shaking movement of the ground

52 ***flood*** (page 20)
a large amount of water that covers an area that was dry before

53 ***buried*** – *to bury something* (page 20)
to put something in the ground and cover it with earth

54 ***archeologist*** (page 20)
someone who studies ancient societies by looking at the things they left behind, such as the ruins of their buildings and pieces of objects they used

55 ***successful*** (page 21)
a *successful* country (or business) makes a lot of money and has a lot of power

56 ***government*** (page 21)
the people who control a country or area and make decisions about its laws and taxes

57 ***renovated*** – *to renovate something* (page 25)
to make something old look new again by repairing and improving it

58 ***architect*** (page 25)
someone whose job is to design buildings

59 ***shore*** (page 25)
the land that is on the edge of a sea or lake
60 ***troops*** (page 25)
soldiers
61 ***World's Fair*** (page 26)
a public event where countries show their industrial products and technology
62 ***die out*** – *to die out* (page 27)
to gradually disappear or stop existing
63 ***achievement*** (page 28)
a difficult thing he succeeded in doing
64 ***automatic timing device*** (page 29)
a piece of equipment that measures time. It is started automatically by the signal for the start of the race.
65 ***public-address system*** (page 29)
a piece of electrical equipment for making announcements or for playing music in a public place
66 ***double*** (page 31)
twice as many
67 ***screen*** (page 32)
a flat surface where a film is shown. You also have a screen on a computer, television or other piece of electronic equipment.
68 ***billion*** (page 33)
the number 1,000,000,000
69 ***bravery*** (page 33)
behaviour that shows that you are *brave* – able to deal with danger, pain or trouble without being frightened or worried
70 ***long-distance*** (page 34)
moving between two places that are far apart
71 ***fibreglass*** (page 34)
a light hard substance made from very thin pieces of glass
72 ***score*** (page 35)
the number of points that someone gains in a game or competition
73 ***amputee*** (page 39)
someone who has had a part of their body cut off in a medical operation
74 ***cancelled*** – *to cancel something* (page 39)
to decide that something that has been arranged will not now happen

75 ***collarbone*** (page 39)
the bone along the front of your shoulder, at the bottom of your neck

76 ***wheelchair*** (page 39)
a chair with large wheels that someone who cannot walk uses for moving around

77 ***celebrity*** (page 40)
a famous entertainer or sports personality

78 ***entertained*** – *to entertain someone* (page 40)
to give a performance that people enjoy

79 ***Nazi*** (page 41)
someone who belonged to the political party that governed Germany before and during the Second World War

80 ***Jewish*** (page 41)
someone who is Jewish was born in the Jewish culture and may practise *Judaism* – the religion based on the writings of the Torah and the Talmud

81 ***army camp*** (page 42)
a place where soldiers live during a war

82 ***boycott*** – *to boycott something* (page 43)
to protest about something by not taking part in an event or not buying certain products

83 ***invasion*** (page 43)
an occasion when one country's army goes into another country in order to take control of it

84 ***Soviet*** (page 43)
relating to the former Union of Soviet Socialist Republics (USSR), the group of Communist states in Russia and Eastern Europe until 1991

85 ***triumph*** (page 44)
an exciting victory or success

86 ***struggle*** (page 44)
an attempt to do something that takes a lot of effort over a period of time

87 ***official*** (page 44)
someone with an important position in an organization

88 ***cheated*** – *to cheat* (page 44)
to behave dishonestly or to not obey the rules to try to win. Someone who does this is called a *cheat*.

89 ***fine*** (page 45)
an amount of money that you must pay because you have cheated or disobeyed the rules

90 ***sword*** (page 45)
a weapon with a short handle and a long sharp blade

91 ***disqualified*** – *to disqualify someone* (page 45)
to not allow someone to take part in something because they have cheated or done something wrong

92 ***terrorist*** (page 46)
someone who uses violence in order to achieve political aims

93 ***hostage*** (page 46)
a person who is the prisoner of someone who threatens to kill them if they do not get what they want

94 ***memorial service*** (page 46)
an event that is organized to honour people who have died

95 ***bomb*** (page 46)
a weapon that is made to explode at a particular time or when it hits something

96 ***injury*** (page 48)
physical harm done to a person or a part of their body

97 ***visually impaired*** (page 49)
not fully able to see

98 ***cerebral palsy*** (page 49)
a medical condition that affects someone's ability to control their movement and speech

99 ***intellectual*** (page 50)
relating to someone's ability to think and understand things

100 ***publicity*** (page 52)
advertisements and other attention at events and in newspapers and on television

101 ***television rights*** (page 53)
the legal authority to show something on television

102 ***communications*** (page 53)
systems for sending information

103 ***broadcaster*** (page 53)
a person or company that makes and sends out programmes on radio, television and the Internet

104 ***technology*** (page 54)
machines and equipment that are developed using advanced scientific knowledge

105 ***motto*** (page 54)
a short statement that expresses a principle or aim

Exercises

Background Information

Read the statements about the Olympics. Write T (True) or F (False).

1 The Summer and Winter Olympics are in the same country. ......*F*......

2 The Youth Olympics were first held in 2010. ....

3 The Olympic Games are about a thousand years old. ....

4 The host country chooses the mascot. ....

5 The Olympic torch arrives at the end of the Games. ....

6 The Greek team always starts the parade. ....

7 They play the same song at the beginning of every Games. ....

8 The Olympics continue for about a week. ....

9 The IOC gives the flag to the next host country at the end of the Games. ....

10 The ancient Olympics began in Athens in Greece. ....

11 Ancient Greece was a peaceful country. ....

12 In the ancient Olympics, there were men's and women's teams.
....

Important People

Complete the gaps. Use each name in the box once.

Demetrious Vikelas	Evangelis Zappas	Georgios Averoff
Panagiotis Soutsos	Pierre de Coubertin	~~William Penny Brookes~~

1 *William Penny Brookes* organized England's first Olympic Games in London.

2 An architect called .... gave money to renovate a stadium in Athens.

3 When .... died, all his money went to pay for a modern Olympic Games.

4 .... believed the Olympics would help Greece become important again.

5 The first president of the International Olympics Committee was ....

6 .... wanted different countries to take part in the Olympics.

Important Dates

Write a date from the box next to the correct information below.

1920 1906 1936 1896 1924 ~~456 BC~~
1928 1956 1908 1904

1 The Temple of Zeus was built at Olympia. 456 BC

2 The first modern IOC Olympic Games were held. ....

3 They held an extra, unofficial, Olympic Games in Athens. ....

4 They gave gold, silver and bronze medals for the first time. ....

5 At the closing ceremony, the athletes all came in together. ....

6 The marathon was made longer so that it went past a castle. ....

7 They used the Olympic flag and the Oath for the first time. ....

8 The first Winter Olympics were held in France. ....

9 Women could compete in gymnastics and track and field events.

....

10 The Olympics were shown on large television screens in the city.

....

Vocabulary: Sports words

Complete the table. Write the sports words in the box in the correct column.

bobsledding canoeing ~~discus~~ hurdles ice-skating javelin long jump ~~luge~~ pole vault rowing ~~running~~ sailing skiing swimming team relays walking ~~water polo~~

Track events	Field events	Water sports	Winter sports
running	*discus*	*water polo*	*luge*

Now match sports 1–9 to Olympians a–i.

1 running → e	a Bob Beamon
2 javelin	b Jim Thorpe
3 long jump	c Uwe Hohn
4 pentathlon	d Johnny Weissmuller
5 gymnastics	e Jesse Owens
6 swimming	f Charles Vinci
7 canoeing	g Nadia Comăneci
8 shooting	h Birgit Fischer
9 weightlifting	i Károly Takács

Vocabulary: Odd one out

Tick the word which is different.

1 Words connected to the opening and closing ceremonies
- **a** parade
- **b** anthem
- **c** fibreglass ✓
- **d** pigeon

2 Words connected to prizes for the winners
- **a** crown
- **b** statue
- **c** medal
- **d** branches

3 Words connected to disability and the Paralympics
- **a** amputee
- **b** cerebral palsy
- **c** visually impaired
- **d** collarbone

4 Military words – words connected to soldiers and wars
- **a** army camps
- **b** troops
- **c** judge
- **d** bomb

5 Words for groups of people
- **a** committee
- **b** government
- **c** Emperor
- **d** Romans

6 Words connected to cheating
- **a** slaves
- **b** fine
- **c** drugs
- **d** disqualify

Vocabulary: Anagrams

Write the letters in the correct order to make words from the story.

1	TOYBOCT	*boycott*	to refuse to do something because you disagree with it
2	REDSTOY		to damage something so badly it cannot be used
3	RITEBECILES		famous people
4	SETTORRIRS		people who use violence for political reasons
5	GATOSHE		someone who is held for money or political change
6	JURYIN		damage to your body from an accident or violence
7	LIBUPCITY		information about something on TV or in a newspaper
8	GHIRTS		freedom to do things without fear or punishment
9	CANTIEN		very very old
10	DROMEN		new and in the present not the past
11	PHIMURT		success
12	GLERSTUG		to try very hard to do something difficult

Now complete the gaps. Use words from the exercise on page 72.

1 Some countries started to ....*boycott*.......... the Olympic Games in the 1950s.

2 The .... Games have grown and there are many more events than before.

3 The Olympic Games first started in .... Greece.

4 Many famous people and .... wanted to support the Olympic Games.

5 Some athletes performed when they had an ....

6 The worst time for the Olympics was when some .... attacked one of the teams.

7 Some companies advertise their products at the Olympics, which is good .... for them.

Vocabulary: Collocations

Complete the table. Write the words in the box in the correct column.

archery baseball croquet football ~~gymnastics~~ ice hockey judo taekwondo volleyball weightlifting

do	*play*
gymnastics	

Word Focus

Complete the table with the correct form of the words.

Noun	Verb	Adjective
bravery	–	*brave*
achievement		–
	celebrate	–
	–	independent
competition		
		disappointed
	invade	–
injury		
	succeed	
		organized

Complete the sentences with one of the words from the table.

1 Some athletes are very *disappointed* if they don't win a medal.

2 All the athletes work really hard to .... in the Games.

3 Fireworks are often part of the .... at the end of the Olympics.

4 Károly Takács learnt to shoot with his left hand when his right hand was ....

5 Jim Thorpe was .... in both the pentathlon and decathlon events.

6 An .... called the IOC chooses where to hold the Olympics.

Grammar: Comparatives and superlatives

Choose the correct form to complete the sentences.

1 Before the 1908 Games, the marathon was more short / shorter.

2 In 1924 the Olympic Games were biger / bigger than in 1896.

3 In 1936 Jesse Owens was the faster / the fastest runner in the stadium.

4 They took the Olympic torch up the most high / the highest mountain.

5 Modern javelins are more heavily / heavier than before.

6 Many people come to see the better / the best athletes in the world.

7 They think pole vaulting is easier / easyer than the long jump.

8 She is exciteder / more excited about winning than losing.

9 It is getting more expensive / expensiver to hold the Olympics.

10 Every year the athletes try to do better / the best than everyone else.

11 Who will win the more / the most medals?

Grammar: The present perfect

Use the words and phrases to make sentences in the present perfect.

1 Some countries / lose / money.

Some countries have lost money.

2 The Games / become / shorter.

3 Some of the equipment / change.

4 The Paralympics / become / more popular.

5 The cost of hosting the Olympics / increase.

....

6 Many athletes / become / famous.

....

Grammar: The present perfect passive

Use the words and phrases to make passive sentences in the present perfect.

1 More money / spend / on security.

More money has been spent on security.

2 The photo-finish / introduce.

....

3 Women / allow / to compete.

....

4 More events / added.

....

5 More records / broke.

....

6 Some athletes / disqualified.

....

Pronunciation: Vowel sounds

Look at the underlined letters. Decide what vowel sounds they are then write the words in the correct column of the table.

ancient anthem archeologist archery architect
~~army~~ athlete branches celebrations chariot invasion
~~slaves~~ stadium statue ~~track~~

/ɑː/	/æ/	/eɪ/
army	*track*	*slaves*

Pronunciation: Syllable stress

Write the words in the correct column of the table.

architect celebrate celebrity ~~chariot~~ disappointment
independent intellectual invasion memorial publicity
spectator successful weightlifting

●••	•●•	•●••	••●•
chariot			

Macmillan Education
4 Crinan Street
London N1 9XW
A division of Springer Nature Limited
Companies and representatives throughout the world

ISBN 978-1-3800-4174-6
ISBN 978-1-3800-4111-1 (with CD edition)

First published 2012
This edition published 2019

Designed by Carolyn Gibson
Cover photograph by Getty Images/The Image Bank/David Madison

The authors and publishers would like to thank the following for permission to reproduce their photographs: **Alamy**/Archive pics p24, Alamy/Hemis p14, Alamy/E.Langsley Olympic Images p10; **Allsport** p49; **Corbis**/Bettmann p41; **De Agostini Picture Library** p16; **Mary Evans Picture Library** p18; **Getty Images**/AFP/JAVIER SORIANO p10, Getty Images/Stringer/China Photos p32, Getty Images Sport p30; **Hulton Archive** pp42, 47; **Rex Features** p12, Rex Features/Alinari p36, Rex Features/P.Hillyard/Newspix p37, Rex Features/Sipa Press pp32, 51, Rex Features/KPA/Zuma p53.

Printed and bound in United Kingdom by Bell and Bain Ltd, Glasgow

without CD edition

2023 2022 2021 2020 2019
10 9 8 7 6 5 4 3 2 1

with CD edition

2023 2022 2021 2020 2019
10 9 8 7 6 5 4 3 2 1